Bear was the best bubble blower on his block.
Bear could blow great big bubbles.

Bear could blow itsy-bitsy bubbles.

Bear could even blow a bubble beard!

Bear could blow lots of bubble shapes, too.

Bear could blow a bubble bell

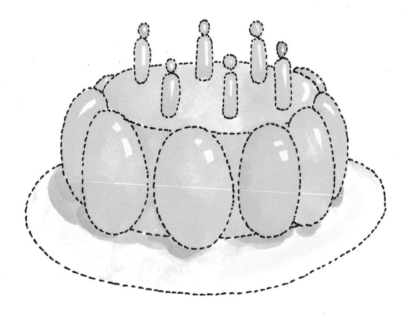

and a bubble birthday cake

and a bubble bunny

and, of course, a bubble bear!

One day, Badger saw Bear blowing bubbles.
Badger was a bully.
Everyone on the block was afraid of her.

"Only babies blow bubbles," Badger told Bear.
But Bear kept right on blowing.
He blew and blew until he had blown...

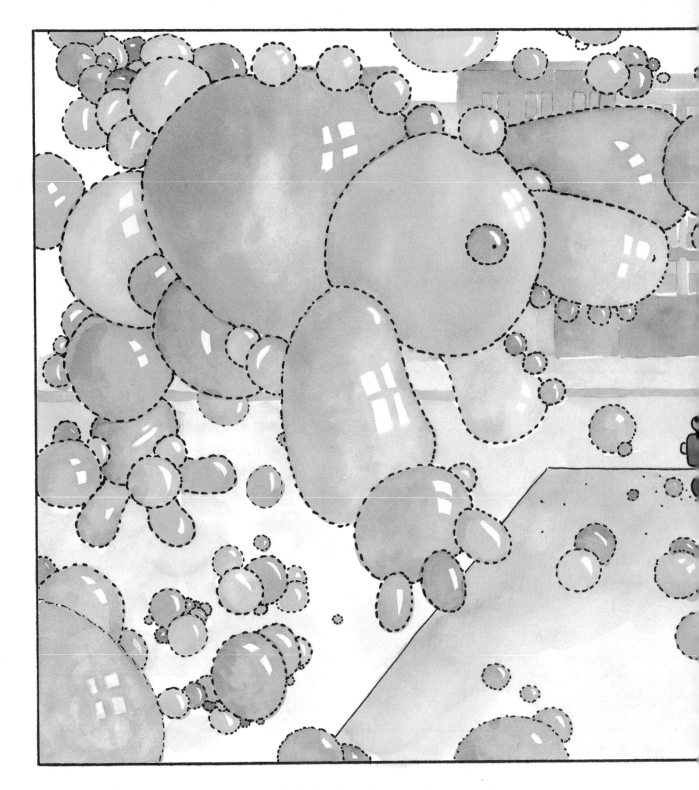

...a great big bubble beast!

"Ahhhhh!" yelled Badger.
She ran behind a bush.

"Only babies are afraid of bubbles!"
Bear told Badger.

"Bear, I am sorry I called you a baby,"
said Badger. "Will you show me how you blow
such beautiful bubbles?"

So Bear showed Badger how to blow big bubbles and itsy-bitsy bubbles. He showed her how to blow a bubble beard, a bubble bell, and a bubble birthday cake.

He showed her how to blow a bubble
bunny, a bubble bear, and a bubble badger.
And Bear even showed Badger how to blow
a great big bubble beast!

See inside back cover for answers.

Bb Cheer

B is for bear, bubbles, and boat

B is for buttons on your coat

B is for bicycle, bunny, and bat

B is for bee—imagine that!

Hooray for **B**, big and small—

The best, most beautiful letter of all!